THE NEW PERSPECTIVE ON JUSTIFICATION
A Brief Introduction to the Discussion

Steve West

THE NEW PERSPECTIVE ON JUSTIFICATION
A Brief Introduction to the Discussion

Steve West

NEW **C**OVENANT MEDIA

5317 Wye Creek Drive, Frederick, MD 21703-6938
phone: 301-473-8781 or 800-376-4146 fax: 240-206-0373
email: info@newcovenantmedia.com
Website: www.newcovenantmedia.com

THE NEW PERSPECTIVE ON JUSTIFICATION
A Brief Introduction to the Discussion

Copyright 2011 © by Steve West.

Published by:

New Covenant Media
5317 Wye Creek Drive
Frederick, Maryland 21703-6938
Orders: www.newcovenantmedia.com

Printed in the United States of America

ISBN 13: 978-1-928965-37-4

Dedication

To:
My wife
Heather,
and daughters
Charlotte and Brooklyn

Contents

Introduction

The subtitle of this booklet really does convey my intention. This is neither "A Brief Defense" of the new perspective, nor is it "A Brief Critique." Both defenses and critiques of the new perspective are not in short supply these days (although brevity certainly is!). There does seem to be a significant lack, however, in entry points into the discussion. This is not the last word, but it is hopefully a useful first word, which will provide a point of departure for more careful study.

When someone begins to study an unfamiliar topic, it is a principle of research that they are supposed to start with a general work, and move from there to more specific works. For example, an encyclopedia article provides an overview of a topic, while a scholarly journal article provides an in-depth discussion on technical matters. If you have never studied a given topic before, the journal article is not the place to start because it presupposes that you already have a basic grasp of the topic. It may contain many excellent insights, but until you understand the fundamentals of your subject, you will probably not understand or appreciate the insights the article contains. Studying general works first and progressing to more specific and technical works as you grow in your understanding is the way to most effectively learn.

In my judgment, the vast majority of literature about the new perspective is technical and heavy. This is very, very understandable, given the issues and level of debate. However, the new perspective is not remaining purely in the scholarly domain where such writing and argumentation is expected. I personally know pastors and missionaries who are very receptive to this new view of justification. In a discussion after church one morning, it also came to my attention that there are people in my congregation who are reading Don Carson, John Piper, and N. T. Wright about justification. The discussion about the new perspective is not only at the scholar's lectern; it is not only in the pulpit; it is also in the pew.

As a pastor, I want the congregation to read the best theology by the best scholars. Over time, however, I have come to suspect that most people in the congregation are not going to spend several weeks pouring over both volumes of *Justification and Variegated Nomism*, the works of N. T. Wright, Dunn's journal articles, and all the rest. The literature is immense, technical, and *expensive*. Piper and Wright have now offered up more popular level works, but they are still hardly an easy read for those who are completely unfamiliar with the topic. This goes for pastors as well. The pressures and constraints of pastoral ministry are well known, and it is sheer fantasy to imagine that pastors have the liberty to buy, read, and digest all the literature they want on all the issues they want. What is needed, in my opinion, is a relatively short and concise entry point to the discussion, and I hope that this booklet serves that purpose.

There are advantages and disadvantages to any approach. One of the weaknesses in a small work like this is that the supporting argumentation will be short-changed. Conclusions will be noted, but most of the reasoning will be passed over in silence. Or, one or two key points may be noted, but it needs to be understood that these points are also the subject of supporting arguments. The reader needs to be aware that there are long chains of data and reasoning underlying the general positions cited, but such reasoning clearly cannot be identified (let alone analyzed) in a short introductory piece.

The greatest risk in a project like this is caricature, *but that is one thing I am trying very hard to avoid.* Even when positions are oversimplified, I hope it is not to the point of complete distortion. Anyone engaging in further study will tidy up the lack of nuance.

Unfair Arguments

Before examining some of the issues involved in the new perspective on justification, it may be profitable to remind ourselves of some types of arguments which are unfair, illogical, and irrelevant in all rational discussion (and especially *Christian* discussion). I will begin with a personal anecdote, because it will reveal how my own biases have tripped me up in the past, and also because it just happens to be a perfect illustration of completely unfair reasoning. Some time ago when I had been an assistant pastor for a year or two, I was talking to an individual after our church service one evening. Although I do not remember exactly how it came up, the conversation included me making some negative comments on the new perspective. To tell the truth, I had never read a word about it. I could not explain it. I did not know the names of the main proponents, what their arguments were, or really anything about it at all. Perhaps the best way to describe my position was pure ignorance.

Because I was ignorant in both meanings of the word, however, I had no difficulty making some disparaging remarks about the new perspective. The individual I was talking with had no problem seeing how foolish I was being, and gently probed to determine how much I really knew. My crowning remark was: "I don't know very much about the new perspective on justification, but my understanding is that it's new, and there was nothing wrong with the old view!" How utterly embarrassing!

There are many lessons to be learned from conversations like that (some of which revolve around folly, pride, the tongue, wanting to impress, and falling on your face). There are also many questions to be asked. For example, why was I so completely against a position I did not understand? My response was a classic example of a knee-jerk reaction. Perhaps I am not the only one who has reacted that way, with just as little knowledge.

Historically, my response was a repudiation of the very Reformation principles I would have been zealous to maintain. While the tangles of Catholic theology around the time of the Reformation are more diverse than normally admitted, the fact is that at times Luther himself faced the exact same type of reaction concerning his "new" perspective. Those of us who look to Luther as a theological hero and who cannot believe that some people would put tradition over Scripture, need to make sure that our tradition does not cloud the Word of God. The watchwords are *"sola scriptura,"* not *"What did Luther say?"* We cannot dismiss the new perspective simply on the basis that it is not the "old" Reformation perspective.

Furthermore, there are many, many things on which I think Luther, and Calvin for that matter, were dead wrong. I am a Reformed Baptist, not a Lutheran or a Presbyterian. I do not give full consent to the Augsburg Confession or the Westminster Confession. I have read much more Calvin than Luther, but from my reading of them I simply disagree with much of what they say (the same goes for my reading of the early church fathers). Now there is, of course, a tremendous amount that they say which I accept with great joy! Nevertheless, the fact that the Reformers said something does not make it true, nor does it make it binding on the heart and mind of the Christian. Tradition and church history are important, but they are not authoritative.

Theological hero worship is not limited to figures from church history. There is also a very real danger that we will identify our contemporary champions and simply accept whatever their judgments happen to be. For example, I will pick D. A. Carson, because I have been blessed incredibly by his speaking and writing, and he is, frankly, brilliant. Someone else has sat under N. T. Wright, however, and profited from his books, lectures, and wisdom. So, naturally, they pick him as their hero. What happens when my Carson and their Wright conflict? My default position is that I will go with Carson, while their default position is that they will go with Wright. It is wonderful and necessary to have teachers that we respect, but we must place ourselves under the ultimate authority of the Word of God. Incidentally, I have suspected that if we made people read theology *with the authors' names removed from the books*, there would be a crisis of confidence in many places; after all, we wouldn't know which the work of our champion was, and so we wouldn't know what the "right" position was that we were supposed to believe!

There is another bad argument lurking in the same neighborhood of "tradition." Whenever there is a "new" position or practice, invariably the charge is leveled that those who accept it "just love novelty." Psychoanalyzing our opponents this way is not only unfair; it is also atrociously arrogant. Sometimes the claim is even more subversive: perhaps, it is suggested, so-and-so just wants to get famous, and this is why they are propagating this position.

Not only is this style of dismissal uncharitable, it is also illogical. Yes, there are some people who are thrilled with novelty. Yes, there are some people who are trying to be "somebody," and are trying to carve out a theological reputation. But there are also people who love "tradition." There are people who are set in their ways, who think they alone have wisdom, and who cannot even imagine that their cherished views are not 100% correct. What about those who have made *their* reputation as tireless defenders and preachers of the Reformation perspective on justification? It would be exceptionally difficult to admit that after decades of preaching one had been wrong about a central doctrine and that many sermons had been based on the misinterpretation of key texts. Let us not allow ourselves to think that one side is only novelty and pride, or that the other is only traditionalism and pride. Such thinking is neither kind nor rational.

Is discovering new truth about Scripture exciting? Of course it is. Even when the theology is wrong, there is an excitement that attends learning something new. Some people have been thrilled to learn the 'truth' about Revelation from Hal Lindsey or the *Left Behind Series.* Others have been thrilled to learn about the doctrines of grace, or believer's baptism, or, for that matter, open theism. In other words, whether the doctrine is right or wrong (lest I be misunderstood, open theism is the latter), it is exciting when we *think* it is right. I have heard many lovers of the doctrines of grace tell me how excited they were to learn these new truths—for them, gaining a new perspective on something as critical as soteriology was a wonderful, exciting experience.

Gaining new vantage points or new "perspectives" is something that can be thrilling for all. I remember the first time I actually studied the book of Genesis, and the familiar Sunday school stories came alive with depths that I had never imagined existed. This was a very exciting study for me. I had a new appreciation, a new perspective on Genesis. After all, the word *perspective* is quite ambiguous. For my study in Genesis, I could say that I gained a whole new perspective on the book. But, in reality, it was only a deeper understanding. I did not, for example, move from being an atheist to a Christian on the basis of the study, or move from thinking Genesis was pure fiction to thinking it was historically accurate. There are changes in perspective which can bring to light a previously obscured facet of a topic, and then there are changes in perspective which are revolutionary and Copernican in nature. Two perspectives may complement each other perfectly, or they may be in total opposition and contradiction.

Lastly, we need more intellectual humility. It can be hard for pastors (myself included) to admit that the limits of our knowledge are actually very small. I remember a friend and colleague remarking that he didn't know "the literature of Second Temple Judaism from a hole in the ground." May we all be willing to admit that, if it happens to be true! Sometimes there is a pressure for pastors to know everything. But before waxing eloquent on the extra-canonical literature of Second Temple Judaism, be honest: have you read any of it? Not just a few quotes here and there, but have you read full books? Beyond that, have you studied it well enough to discern the themes and tensions, the points of unity and diversity? The fact that we have heard of the Dead Sea Scrolls and the Qumran Community does not mean that we are familiar with the literature, let alone that we are experts. This does not entail an inability to understand justification: after all, the New Testament *is* literature of Second Temple Judaism! But we do need to recognize upfront the areas in which we are not scholars, so that we can be honest with others and ourselves. However, we must also never forget that *anyone with a Bible has the gospel and all the information they need to understand God's plan of salvation.* Nobody needs the Bible plus Carson, or the Bible plus Sanders, to get the key to justification; all they need is the Bible plus the Spirit of God.

The New Perspective

Before proceeding, a note on resources and citations may be helpful. Since this is a general, introductory work, there will be no footnotes. Piper has written a popular level book on justification which consists of a critique of N. T. Wright, to which Wright has responded with a popular level work of his own. James Dunn has published a collection of his essays and articles in one volume so that the reader can get a survey of his thought, and Don Garlington has published a book in which he brings together some of his essays and reviews on the new perspective. To make referencing easier, these works will be cited by page number alone, without specifying the original article in which the material appeared (bibliographic detail is on the Works Cited page). For the two volume set *Justification and Variegated Nomism*, I will cite the article's author and page number, with the abbreviation *JVN*, and then either 1 or 2 to specify the volume number (e.g., Carson writes "…" *JVN2*). While it would be useful to draw citations from a wide variety of literature, I believe that intentionally staying with a smaller pool of resources which are more summative and synthetic will prove more helpful for the purposes of this brief introduction.

Structurally, this booklet will present the unique contributions of Sanders, Dunn, and Wright. After this, various responses to their work will be presented. It does need to be mentioned that Sanders, Dunn, and Wright are by no means in perfect agreement about everything they write. In fact, they disagree about some fairly major issues. Nevertheless, there is a common core to their work which allows them to be identified as belonging in the camp of the new perspective. Those who are against the new perspective are no more in uniform agreement on every issue than their debating partners. This introduction will attempt, however, to leave idiosyncratic views off to the side, and focus on the central, core areas of agreement on each side.

E. P. Sanders

The seminal work of Sanders entitled *Paul and Palestinian Judaism* (1977) is the place to begin when surveying the literature on the new perspective. For evangelical purposes, Sanders' interpretations of Second Temple Judaism are far more important than his interpretations of Paul. One can reject some of his conclusions concerning Paul, while still needing to wrestle with the implications of the historical, cultural, and theological framework in which Paul was operating. In other words, even if Sanders misreads Paul, this does not mean that traditional Reformation readings of Paul are accurate. It is logically possible that everyone has misread Paul to some extent, and that a greater understanding of the literature of Second Temple Judaism can help provide a missing piece to the puzzle. A mistaken deduction does not mean that the premise is inaccurate!

Regardless of what we do with Paul, Sanders contends that Judaism was simply not a religion of works-righteousness where individuals tried to earn a right standing with God on the basis of their own effort and goodness. The stereotypical Christian view of the Pharisees as people who were proud of their own merited holiness, and who trusted that their salvation hinged on their own established moral righteousness, does not line up with the literature produced by these same religious people. In the end, Christians have caricatured Judaism as a religion where personal righteousness was built up piece by piece, or where individuals sought to pull themselves up by their own moral bootstraps, but this caricature does not comport with reality. Historical Judaism, especially around the time of Jesus and Paul, has been the victim of a radical, misleading, and harmful distortion.

Sanders investigates how the Jewish religion functioned. He writes (1977; 17):

> A pattern of religion, defined positively, is the description of how a religion is perceived by its adherents to *function*. 'Perceived to function' has the sense not of what an adherent does on a day-to-day basis, but of *how getting in and staying in are understood*: the way in which a religion is understood to admit and retain members is considered to be the way it 'functions' (emphasis in original).

Studying "function" in this sense is a reasonable approach for grasping the basic contours of a religion. Does the religion teach that an individual "gets in" on the basis of their own hard moral effort, or does the religion teach that people get in on the basis of sheer grace? Does the religion teach that, once in, the individual can do anything they want and still receive temporal and eternal blessings, or does the religion teach that you can "lose your salvation" if you do not work hard enough, offer the right sacrifices, say the right prayers, or the like? Can you forfeit your covenant status? The particular ways of phrasing the questions could run on at length, but the main point is clear.

How did Israelites "get in"? Israelites did not earn their way in; they were born in. As the covenant people of God, with circumcision as the sign of the covenant, they were literally born into the covenant community. "Getting in" to the covenant community was a matter of birth. It hardly needs to be observed that being born is not exactly a meritorious, righteousness-earning activity. While some Rabbis did teach that Israel had been given the covenant itself because of merit, it was their view that in their own day covenant membership was not merited (Sanders, 1977; 104). "Getting in" was not a matter of merit or a matter of earning one's way; it was a matter of God's elective grace.

What is undeniable about the Jewish view of the law, however, was that it was to be strictly obeyed. If law-keeping or personal moral goodness and effort did not earn one's way into the covenant people, why were the Rabbis so concerned with obeying the law? Sanders argues that the Jews painstakingly kept the law not in an attempt to earn merit with God but as a proper response to God for his including them in the covenant (pp. 81-82). Obedience demonstrated love for God (p. 83). It was because they were already "in" that they wanted to keep the law. Such obedience entailed rewards, but the rewards were not the motivation for obeying (p. 83). Beyond this, however, the law is not something that is obeyed to gain entrance into the covenant, but it is *the condition of remaining in it* (p. 94 fn 40, emphasis in original).

At this point the requirements of "getting in" and "staying in" are clarified. Rabbis did not teach that one got in by obeying the law, but they did teach that one *stayed in* by obeying the law. Obedience was a sign of gratitude and love for God, but it was also necessary to keep one's covenant position or membership. The covenant and the law could not be separated. As Sanders (p. 134) writes: "Since accept-

ing the covenant meant accepting the commandments, refusal of the commandments is refusal of the covenant." Or,
in other words (pp. 146-147): "Obedience and the intention
to obey are required if one is to remain in the covenant and
share in its promises, but they do not earn God's mercy."
Once more (p. 180): "The intention and effort to be obedient
constitute the *condition for remaining in the covenant*, but they
do not *earn* it" (emphasis in original).

While this position is clear, it does raise an interesting
question: What level of obedience is required to stay in? Did
the covenant demand a full life of perfect obedience or else
the individual was out of the covenant? Was there an acceptable quota of sins that could be committed before one
was removed? Could acts of supererogation make up for
large numbers of rebellious deeds? Starting on the basis of
God's mercy and election is one thing, but if the individual
is then left to maintain a sinless perfection in order to remain
in the covenant—well, how many could seriously imagine
they would qualify?

Sanders argues that nobody expected to perfectly fulfill
the law. This was actually based on the law itself: since
atonement was provided for sins, it was obvious that sins
would be committed. Repentance was called for, and
atonement available for every sin in the covenant (p. 147).
The only sin for which atonement was not possible was ab-
solute apostasy, since this entailed rejecting God and the
covenant in which the provisions for atonement were made.
In Rabbinic Judaism (p. 157): "The universally held view is
this: God has appointed means of atonement for every
transgression, except the intention to reject God and his cov-

enant." In terms of getting in and staying in, Sanders (p. 178) explains:

> Thus repentance is not a 'status-achieving' activity by which one initially courts and wins the mercy of God. It is a 'status-maintaining' or 'status-restoring' attitude which indicates that one intends to remain in the covenant. To use other language, one is already 'saved'; what is needed is the maintenance of a right attitude toward God. Without it, the mercy of God is of no avail. One enters the covenant by accepting God's offer of it; one remains in it by continuing to accept it; and this implies repentance for transgressions.

Since the covenant is maintained by desiring to remain within it, by obedience, and by repentance for sins, it is obvious that sinless perfection was simply not imagined to be necessary to stay in the covenant. There are built-in guidelines and provisions to deal with sin committed by a covenant member.

This basic pattern of religion is termed *covenantal nomism* by Sanders. The religion functions in terms of "getting in" to the *covenant* by mercy and birth, and by "staying in" the covenant by keeping the law (*nomism*). While not pretending to have conducted an exhaustive survey of every extant writing of Second Temple Judaism, Sanders (p. 75) does believe that he has studied widely and representatively enough to conclude that: "The all-pervasive view can be summarized in the phrase 'covenantal nomism'. Briefly put, covenantal nomism is the view that the covenant requires as the proper response of man his obedience to its commandments, while providing means of atonement for transgression."

In summarizing his study of the literature of Second Temple Judaism, Sanders (p. 422) concludes:

> The 'pattern' or 'structure' of covenantal nomism is this: (1) God has chosen Israel and (2) given the law. The law implies both (3) God's promise to maintain the election and (4) the requirement to obey. (5) God rewards obedience and punishes transgression. (6) The law provides for means of atonement, and atonement results in (7) maintenance or re-establishment of the covenantal relationship. (8) All those who are maintained in the covenant by obedience, atonement and God's mercy belong to the group which will be saved. An important interpretation of the first and last points is that election and ultimately salvation are considered to be by God's mercy rather than human achievement.

This covenantal nomism, according to Sanders, was pervasive in the time of Jesus and Paul, and must have been the dominant and most common type of religion in Palestine (p. 426). As such, it is historically inaccurate to say that Judaism was a religion where individuals trusted in their own works to secure or earn righteousness. Furthermore, their own works fell short of maintaining a perfect works-righteousness, which is why atonement and repentance were necessary for maintaining their covenant status. The terms of the covenant could be fulfilled because of God's merciful provision for human failing. Salvation, in this understanding, was owing to the mercy of God rather than human moral effort and goodness.

While Sanders's views on Paul are interesting and worthy of study (see Sanders 1977; 429-523: also see Sanders *Paul* 2009), they are not particularly relevant to the purpose of this booklet (and they do not fit in its scope). In my estimation, Sanders's interpretations of Paul are not as influential in evangelicalism as other interpretations of Paul which are based in part on Sanders's work on the extra-canonical literature of Second Temple Judaism. Some scholars are mainly in agreement with Sanders until they get to Paul, at which point they diverge in a different direction. Sanders may very well have brought a new perspective on Second Temple Judaism, while others have gone on to be the leading proponents of the new perspective on justification.

James D. G. Dunn

Dunn believes that Sanders has made his case that the Jews started in the covenant, maintained their status through obedience to the law, and could provide atonement for sin (2008; 6). (All page references are from Dunn *The New Perspective on Paul, Revised Edition* 2008). Dunn, however, does not believe that Sanders's handling of Paul is persuasive (p. 7). This means that Dunn is a scholar who accepts Sanders's main thesis concerning Second Temple Judaism, but who then interprets Paul quite differently from both Sanders and traditional Reformation theologians.

After two and a half decades of teaching the new perspective on Paul, Dunn wrote a very helpful essay surveying major developments in the field. He offers a five-point summary of the main contentions of the new perspective (pp. 16-17):

> 1. It builds on Sanders' new perspective on Second Temple Judaism, and Sanders' reassertion of the basic graciousness expressed in Judaism's understanding and practice of covenantal nomism.
>
> 2. It observes that a social function of the law was an integral aspect of Israel's covenantal nomism, where separateness *to* God (holiness) was understood to require separateness *from*

the (other) nations as two sides of the one coin, and that the law was understood as the means to maintaining both.

3. It notes that Paul's own teaching on justification focuses largely if not principally on the need to overcome the barrier which the law was seen to interpose between Jew and Gentile, so that the 'all' of 'to all who believe' (Rom. 1:17) signifies, in the first place, Gentile as well as Jew.

4. It suggests that 'works of law' became a key slogan in Paul's exposition of his justification gospel because so many of Paul's fellow Jewish believers were insisting on certain works as indispensable to their own (and others?) standing within the covenant, and therefore as indispensable to salvation.

5. It protests that failure to recognise this major dimension of Paul's doctrine of justification by faith may have ignored or excluded a vital factor in combating the nationalism and racialism which has so distorted and diminished Christianity past and present.

While Dunn has written an impressive body of scholarly works when it comes to the new perspective, they largely represent a fleshing out of this outline. The next few pages, therefore, will be dedicated to unpacking some of the details involved in these five points.

First, we need to see a few clarifications that Dunn makes, and we need to understand them if we are to avoid setting up a straw man. Dunn (p. 20) is very clear that he accepts justification by grace through faith as the heart of the gospel. He is not attempting to throw out everything the Reformation taught and accomplished, but he is trying to bring out some aspects of justification which were missed by Luther and his followers (p. 23). The social and ethnic dimensions of justification have been overlooked, but pointing this out does not mean that individual salvation is unimportant in justification (p. 30). Rather than refuting the Reformed doctrine, or rejecting the importance of individual salvation, Dunn insists that he is trying to set out the social and ethnic components of justification, which were vitally important to Paul and the church, and which figured prominently in the original, *biblical* formulations of the doctrine of justification (p. 36).

What evidence does Dunn have in support of his claims? Perhaps his most famous exegetical argument revolves around his interpretation of the phrase 'works of law' or 'works of the law.' Dunn identifies these works of law as being very specific: they are representative *boundary markers*. In other words, they are specific items which draw lines of distinction, set up property lines, or mark the boundaries between God's people and everyone else. Or, to put it another way, they are "identity markers" or "badges of covenant membership" (p. 109).

Dunn notes that both Jewish and Gentile writers saw certain characteristics of Judaism as distinctive of the Jewish identity. Particularly, Sabbath observance, refusing to eat pork, and circumcision served as these markers (pp. 108-109). Now, it is essential to recognize one of Dunn's clarifications at this point (pp. 23-24): "Let me make it quite clear, then: I have no doubt that 'works of the law' refer to what the law requires, the conduct prescribed by the Torah; whatever the law requires to be done can be described as 'doing' the law, as a work of the law." In practice, however, certain specific elements of the law came to be recognized, by synecdoche, as representative of the whole. So the phrase 'works of the law' could refer to the whole Torah, but with "special reference to such crucial issues [as circumcision, etc.]" (p. 214).

During the Maccabean revolt, Jews died rather than violate their food laws, and they died rather than refuse to circumcise their sons, as the Seleucid powers demanded. It was not because the food laws were the most important laws, but they were badges which clearly demarcated the Jews from their oppressors. In the literature of the Qumran community, there is also reference to the 'works of the law' or the 'deeds of the law,' and these deeds were what separated the members of the community (i.e., insiders) from outsiders (p. 204). By way of a contemporary example, for some people the ordination of women priests is a touchstone issue or a shibboleth, even though it is hardly the most important aspect of the Christian faith (p. 379). An issue can be secondary, but if it is the proverbial line in the sand, it can figure extremely prominently in all discussions.

In Dunn's judgment, Paul always understood justification to be by faith alone, but he added the negative contrast "not by works of law" only after the incident where Peter withdrew from table fellowship with Gentile Christians (p. 36). Bolstering this analysis is the fact that the phrase 'works of law' is only used in Romans and Galatians, where the issue is how Gentiles can share in the blessings promised to Abraham (p. 461). Dunn (pp. 461-462) writes: "Anticipating a little, we could define 'works of the law' more fully as *what members of the covenant must do in order to attest their membership, to live their life as God's people, to secure acquittal in the final judgment, and* (when thought of life beyond death emerges) *to ensure participation in the life of the age to come*" (emphasis in original).

In order to be part of God's covenant people, then, some believers were insisting that Gentile Christians also had to live behind the boundary markers of the law. The first place Paul writes about the 'works of the law' and justification is in Galatians, exactly where Jews were insisting that Gentile Christians live like them (p. 28). As the apostle to the Gentiles, Paul was formulating his doctrine of justification in the face of opposition that insisted that the laws of Leviticus 20:22-26 which were to keep Israel from mixing with other nations were still in force (pp. 30-31). For some Jews it was simply inconceivable that someone outside the boundaries of the Torah, or someone not wearing the badges, could be part of God's people. Paul's great argument is that (p. 113): "From being *one* identity marker for the Jewish Christian alongside the other identity markers (circumcision, food laws, Sabbath), faith in Jesus as Christ becomes the primary identity marker which renders the others superfluous" (emphasis in original). Paul argues, in other words, that faith in Jesus is the only badge the new covenant community needs to wear. Even Peter himself had to learn in Acts that Cornelius was clean because God made him clean apart from the old boundary markers (p. 31).

Any reader of the Pauline letters can attest to how often circumcision figures in his arguments. In Dunn's estimation (pp. 162-163), this is owing to the socio-theological role boundary markers played:

> In sociological terms, circumcision clearly functioned as a primary and effective identity and boundary marker, particularly for the Jewish minorities in the cities of the Diaspora. It was not the only such marker, but because circumcision was such a distinctive feature within a Hellenistic environment, because it had been so integrally tied into the covenant from the

first, and because it had become such a test-case for national loyalty for all who regarded themselves as heirs of the Maccabean inheritance, it was bound to be *the* mark of the covenant people for most Jews of Paul's time.

This is why Paul's arguments can be so focused on 'those of the circumcision' (pp. 153-154). But it must be understood that faith in God's promises was what justified Abraham, and this was *before* the badge of circumcision was given (Rom. 4). So faith alone, and not the works of the law, is what from the very beginning marked out the people of God (p. 178).

Before moving on to N. T. Wright, there are two more aspects of Dunn's line of thinking which should be mentioned. The first involves the relationship between the works of the law and merit, and the second involves the relationship between works and future justification, or acquittal at the final judgment. As for the first, harmony with Sanders is clear, and as for the second, Dunn tries to walk a tightrope which can easily create misunderstandings.

When it comes to works and merit, Dunn could not be clearer: the works of the law were boundary markers and are nowhere seen as meritorious (p. 111). The works of the law are not something that one does in order to earn favor with God (p. 111). The governing assumption, in line with covenantal nomism, was not that obeying the law earned a positive moral righteousness; rather, since they are in the covenant, if they are faithful to repent when they sin, their sins are not severe enough to forfeit their status (pp. 220-221). Dunn expresses the contrast in the following way (p. 226):

Did Paul think the law could not be obeyed and that Israel's fault was assuming that it could? Or did he think that Israel was going about obeying the law in the wrong way, *by treating the realm of righteousness as exclusively Jewish territory (marked out by works of the law), and thereby failing to recognize the seriousness of their sin and that they (as much as any Gentile) fell under the law's curse?* It will be clear that I think the latter alternative in each case is much closer to the heart of Paul's gospel and theology (emphasis in original).

Thus, in Dunn's estimation, the law was not something which Jews were attempting to keep in order to earn a righteous status; it was, rather, something they obeyed in order to maintain the righteous status that was already theirs by virtue of their covenant membership. And this membership, which should be clearly understood at this point, was demonstrated by certain badges or boundary markers.

Dunn sounds very much like Sanders in this position. Dunn argues that the Judaism of Paul's day was actually not legalistic, and that justification by faith and the grace of God were fundamentally Jewish doctrines (pp. 370-371). In fact (p. 371): "The proposition that relationship with God is first and foremost a gift and not something earned, an act of grace and not reward for merit, would be axiomatic to any Jew who took the Torah and the Prophets seriously." Paul himself, according to Dunn, was not converted from trying to earn his own righteousness before God; instead, he came to see that grace was freely available for all, not just those in Israel's covenant (p. 375). Paul's mistake, therefore, was not that he was trying to earn his own salvation; it was trusting in his special, ethnic covenantal status as represented by the works of the law.

When it comes to the relationship between works and future judgment (or "future justification"), Dunn insists that a final judgment on the basis of works cannot be glossed over or dismissed (p. 426). He maintains that justification is fundamentally futuristic in its orientation (p. 401) and "indicate[s] a process begun but yet to be completed" (p. 402). As a result, it is accurate to say that we are already justified, but also that we will be justified in the future. The tension involves the familiar "already/not yet" distinction. If the language used is that of "salvation," we can say that we "are saved," that we are "being saved," and that we "will be saved." There is a sense in which we are saved now, a sense in which salvation is a process, and a sense in which our future salvation is yet to be. Dunn's position is that the same is true of justification. We are already justified, but have not yet been finally acquitted/justified (p. 402).

Dunn believes that there are many texts which plainly teach that final judgment is based on works (pp. 75-76). These works are done by the power of the Holy Spirit and Christ in us, but it is nevertheless *we* who do them and *we* who are judged (pp. 85-89). This does not mean that final justification is not on the basis of an alien righteousness; for Dunn, not only is this possible, but it is actually the case (p. 85). Still, we are judged by works, and their role is more than just being evidential of the saving work that God has done in us (p. 87 fn 367). But neither is this semi-Pelagian, nor a position which views justification in terms of synergism (pp. 88-89). There may be a tension in Paul, but it was one that he accepted and we have to live with. In the end, we are justified by faith, and judged by our works (p. 89). Dunn (p. 97) expresses the matter this way: "The interrelationship has to be maintained between justification by faith and judgment according to works...The tensions here have been long debated, but the present controversy over the new perspective shows that the debate has still a long way to run."

N. T. Wright

In terms of theology, Wright has a whole, unique paradigm that he is teasing out (which serves as the larger framework in which his discussion of justification is located), but the constraints of the current project are going to make it impossible to even summarize much of his work. Fortunately, having already laid a foundation with Sanders and Dunn, not everything Wright says needs to be examined. Keeping the discussion at an introductory level, it should be sufficient to underscore a few key points.

Wright, although stating that Piper does not understand what he (i.e., Wright) is saying (Wright, *Justification: God's Plan & Paul's Vision* 2009; 21), does not want to deny that Piper and his tradition have a valuable understanding of the gospel. They (p. 10) "have said that salvation is accomplished by the sovereign grace of God, operating through the death of Jesus Christ in our place and on our behalf, and appropriated through faith alone. Absolutely. I agree a hundred percent. There is not a syllable of that summary that I would complain about." So Wright is not—as Dunn is not—trying to throw away everything in the Reformed tradition concerning justification and soteriology.

What needs to happen, however, if Paul is going to be interpreted correctly, is to locate Paul's teachings and doctrines in the unfolding plot of the biblical revelation. Wright (p. 35) states: "It is central to Paul, but almost entirely ignored in perspectives old, new, and otherwise, that *God had a single plan all along through which he intended to rescue the world and the human race, and that this single plan was centered upon the call of Israel, a call which Paul saw coming to fruition in Israel's representative, the Messiah"* (emphasis in original). It is a great mistake, according to Wright (and a mistake that he thinks Piper makes), to read Paul in any other way than in connection with this unfolding single plan, and to see that the Jews of Paul's day saw themselves in full continuity with the Old Testament narrative (p. 59). They were, in light of Daniel's 70 weeks of prophesied exile, calculating when the weeks would be up, and many felt that it would be in their time in the first century (pp. 56-60). Of the utmost importance to understand is that, even though the Jews had returned from Babylon centuries earlier, they were still ruled by overlords, and the 'exile' was continuing (p. 60). It is this controlling historical narrative, rather than an ahistoric personal soteriology, which provides the interpretive framework necessary for understanding Paul (p. 61).

God's righteousness is to be understood in terms of his faithfulness to all his creation, and specifically his covenant (pp. 67, 178). For an individual to be righteous is to be in the right, or faithfully in the covenant people of God, which includes having one's sins forgiven (p. 170). When an individual is pronounced 'justified' in the lawcourt, they are in the right over against another party; they do not receive the righteousness of the judge (p. 68). Thus justification is a pronouncement of righteousness, but not on the grounds of the imputed righteousness of Jesus Christ, as the Reformed tradition teaches (pp. 66-68). Union with Christ is the key to this doctrine; imputation is sub-biblical (p. 142): "That status the Christian possesses is possessed because of that belongingness, that incorporation. This is the great Pauline truth to which the sub-Pauline idea of 'the imputation of Christ's righteousness' is truly pointing." Again, all that 'righteousness' means in the context of the lawcourt is: "*that status that someone has when the court has found in their favor*" (p. 90, emphasis in original). It is only a granted status (p. 91). It is not an imputed righteousness, but a statement that the purpose of the covenant has been accomplished through the Messiah with whom his people are united (p. 206).

Justification, for Wright, is God's declaration that somebody is in the covenant family. Piper in *The Future of Justification* (2007; 53) quotes Wright: " 'Justification' is thus the declaration of God, the just judge, that someone is (a) in the right, that their sins are forgiven, and (b) a true member of the covenant family, the people belonging to Abraham." Justification does not bring you into the covenant family; it is a declaration that you are in it. Covenant membership is *prior* to justification.

Putting the law court and the covenant together is essential if one is to understand Paul, but there is a third strand which also must be added. Wright (p. 100) observes: "The next dimension of the Biblical, more especially the Pauline, doctrine of justification, belongs closely with the others—the lawcourt, the covenant. They cannot be understood without it, nor it without them, nor the exegesis of the key texts without all three. Eschatology completes a triangle." He goes on to explain (p. 101): "Eschatology: the new world had been inaugurated! Covenant: God's promises to Abraham had been fulfilled! Lawcourt: Jesus had been vindicated— and so all those who belonged to Jesus were vindicated as well! And these, for Paul, were not three, but one. Welcome to Paul's doctrine of justification, rooted in the single scriptural narrative as he read it, reaching out to the waiting world." If you are part of God's people in the present, it is the sign that you will be saved in the end (pp. 146-147).

The end times and the present time intersect in justification (p. 239): "For Paul, a stress on 'justification by faith' is always a stress on the *present status of all God's people in anticipation of the final judgment*," (emphasis in original). The future judgment will in some ways be based on works (pp. 183-185). This judgment on the basis of works will not merely be for rewards, but neither by our works are we earning our salvation (pp. 186-192). Obviously, Wright and Dunn see roughly the same tensions in play.

One of Wright's burdens is to make clear that the Holy Spirit, the third person in the Trinity, also has a role in justification. The works which we do are motivated by love, as the Spirit works in us, but it is we who do them (pp. 192-193). Bringing various strands together, Wright (p. 251) summarizes:

> Finally, as is already clear from the above, this lawcourt verdict, implementing God's covenant plan, and all based on Jesus Christ himself, is announced both in the *present*, with the verdict issued on the basis of faith and faith alone, and also in the *future*, on the day when God raises from the dead all those who are already indwelt by the Spirit. The present verdict gives the *assurance that* the future verdict will match it; the Spirit gives the *power through which* that future verdict, when given, will be seen to be in accordance with the life that the believer has then lived (emphasis in original).

Responses

The literature of Second Temple Judaism was the subject of a fresh and intense study edited by D. A. Carson, Peter T. O'Brien, and Mark Seifrid (*Justification and Variegated Nomism*, Volumes 1 & 2). They brought together a team of specialist scholars to examine various types of literature, to determine what pattern of religion or theological distinctives each type contained. In broad terms, the conclusions were both positive and negative towards Sanders and covenantal nomism. Some literature seemed roughly in agreement with it; other literature seemed to contain elements of it, but by no means the whole system; and still more literature seemed against it. To illustrate:

Falk (*JVN1*; 56) finds that some of the prayers he studied fit well with Sanders, but others did not. He says it is like comparing apples, oranges, and bananas, and just calling it all fruit.

Evans (*JVN1*; 72) - The Pseudopigrapha contains works-righteousness and obedience to the law as necessary for justification; does not lend support to Sanders.

Enns (*JVN1*; 97) – Enns writes: "Despite Sanders's arguments, it is still not entirely clear how 'salvation' can be by grace but 'staying saved' is a matter of strict obedience. If salvation can be lost by disobedience – i.e., if obedience is necessary to 'preserve' salvation – in what sense can we say with Sanders that 'salvation *depends* on the grace of God'? How can there be sins unto death when *election* is the basis of salvation?" Furthermore, Enns (pp. 97-98) doubts that the categories of 'getting in' and 'staying in' do justice to the literature.

Kugler (*JVN1*; 189) – the outcome of his study of Testaments is "not entirely favorable to Sanders's thesis." Yet (p. 213) it does offer "qualified support that covenantal nomism was pervasive in Jewish literature."

Spilsbury (*JVN1*; 252) – Josephus offers a different system than covenantal nomism.

Alexander (*JVN1*; 273) – Sanders has "ironed out" the inconsistencies in Rabbinic literature. It can be seen as "works-righteousness" (p. 300) in places, but it is unsystematic. There are many tensions between works, righteousness, grace, and election, and they are never resolved (p. 301).

Hay (*JVN1*; 370) – Covenantal nomism is not represented by Philo.

Bockmuehl (*JVN1*; 412-413) – Qumran not "fundamentally incompatible" with Sanders, although Sanders did not have access to as many documents as are currently available, and his method would not be considered sufficient today. Sanders was not able to see all the theological diversity that is present.

Seifrid (*JVN1*; 434-438) – The way Sanders uses "righteousness" language is far removed from the Scriptures, rabbinic sources, and Qumran.

A fair reader of *JVN1* will notice that many of the authors, in many places, find evidence that lends support to Sanders and covenantal nomism. The same fair reader will also, however, find that many of the authors in many places find covenantal nomism as not fitting very well, not taking into account other data, and simply not being representative of all the subtleties and diversity of the various literature. D. A. Carson wrote a chapter of conclusions and reflections at the end of *JVN1* which has been much maligned as too negative, unfair, tendentious, and unrepresentative of the essayists' contributions. His motives have even been questioned. Nevertheless, his response needs to be considered.

First, Carson states that Sanders is not completely wrong, but he is wrong when he makes covenantal nomism to be the right structure everywhere in all the literature (*JVN1*; 543). He finds covenantal nomism reductionistic and misleading for two reasons:

> 1) "First, deploying this one neat formula across literature so diverse engenders an assumption that there is more uniformity in the literature than there is." (p. 544)

> 2) "Second, and more importantly, Sanders has erected the structure of covenantal nomism as his alternative to merit theology…By putting over against merit theology not grace but covenant theology, Sanders has managed to have a structure that preserves grace in the 'getting in' while preserving works (and frequently some form or other of merit theology) in the 'staying in.' In other words, it is as if Sanders is saying, 'See, we don't have merit theology here; we have covenantal nomism' – but the covenantal nomism he constructs is so flexible that it includes and baptizes a great deal of merit theology." (pp. 544-545)

When it comes to Paul, then, if he is read exclusively against a backdrop of covenantal nomism, his own writing will have to be distorted to fit (p. 548). What this entails, then, is that the work of Sanders sheds light on some elements found in Second Temple Judaism, but it simply does not represent the entire Jewish religion. Covenantal nomism cannot be the controlling framework in which *all* Second Temple Judaism is understood. At the risk of being tendentious myself, even if one is going to reject a lot of the details of Carson's chapter, these main points are not unfair to the chapters of the book.

Interestingly, in Deines' contribution to *JVN1*, the argument is made that there is a common Judaism to be found in the Second Temple period, and it is related to Pharisaic practice and belief (*JVN1*; 447-453). Pharisaic religion primarily reflected a particular relationship to the Torah, in both written form and traditional customs (pp. 492-493). This form of Judaism was the *closest form to that of the common people*, and thus the most widely accepted, practiced, and distributed (pp. 501-503). The New Testament is not basically involved with the Sadducees, and it is certainly not basically involved with the Essenes and the Qumran Community; it is involved with the beliefs of the majority, and these beliefs were Pharisaic (p. 501). Sanders dismisses the role of the Pharisees far too easily (pp. 447-448). When it comes to the historical background: "For the interpretation of the New Testament and for the history of Jesus and of early Christianity, this means that Jesus and Paul engaged the dominant religious movement of their nation (which was at the same time the one closest to them). This is where it must come to light what both had in common and where they differed." Deines concludes that Pharisaic belief, not Sanders's sweeping category of covenantal nomism, was the most common form of Judaic religion in the Second Temple period.

Second Temple Judaism

The second volume of *Justification and Variegated Nomism* attempts to determine what justification means in the New Testament. Was Second Temple Judaism an era when works-righteousness teaching abounded? Yes and no. According to Gathercole (*JVN2*; 150): "...there are numerous references in the Second Temple literature to a Jewish confidence of vindication on the basis of obedience to Torah..." Silva (in what is in my estimation a very important chapter) notes that in Luke 18:9, Jesus tells a parable against "some who trusted in themselves that they were righteous." Silva points out that *Sanders rejects this pericope, claiming that it is inauthentic* (*JVN2*; 245 fn 66). Even if Jesus never said it, however, it is still the case that the writer of Luke, writing in the first century, thought there were some Jews who thought this way (*JVN2*; 245). The same can be said for Ephesians 2:8-9; Paul can be rejected as the original author, but whoever wrote it felt there needed to be a contrast between works-righteousness and salvation by grace through faith (p. 245). Why would Luke and Ephesians contain these sentiments if nobody in Second Temple Judaism was attempting to earn or merit righteousness? Furthermore, on a high view of biblical inspiration, it is the Scriptures which prove the reality: regardless of what people say or *think they believe*, the Bible reveals the genuine beliefs of our hearts. If the Scriptures depict people trusting their own righteousness, then—regardless of their formal theology—that is exactly what they were doing.

Justification: A Forensic Declaration

A major question in *JVN2* is: Does "justification" in the New Testament denote a forensic declaration of righteousness, in the way that the "old" perspective on justification understood that phrase? Seifrid finds that righteousness and justification language in the New Testament literature is in fact forensic (*JVN2*; 52-59). Blocher finds that this is simply in keeping with classical Greek, where justification never means "to make just"; on the contrary it is always bound up with forensics and a judicial verdict (*JVN2*; 493). Carson (2004; 50-51) shares a personal anecdote where he was talking with a classical Greek expert who could not believe that anyone who knew anything about Greek could think that righteousness/justification could mean anything like: "God's declaration that certain people truly belong to the covenant community." The linguistic data, coupled with a more jaundiced view of the propriety of applying covenantal nomism everywhere across the literature of Second Temple Judaism, means that the new perspective interpretation of Paul fails to be well supported. The historical background does not demand another reading of Paul, and the linguistics of the New Testament does not demand any other interpretation besides the forensic, as understood in the traditional, reformational model.

If the antithesis of justification by faith is justification according to the works of the law (and the latter is impossible), it is very important to understand exactly what "the works of the law" means. As was already seen, Dunn takes it as a technical phrase to signify boundary markers or covenant badges. Dunn does acknowledge that the works of the law are deeper than this, but in the Pauline texts he exegetes, he sees the issues involving the narrower boundary markers between the Jews and Gentiles. O'Brien (*JVN2*; 279) finds that Dunn's narrower interpretation cannot do justice to Romans 9:30-10:3 where Israel is trying to establish their righteousness on the basis of works. The problem in this text is not that Israel is relying on their ethnic boundary markers, but that they are trying to earn a positive righteousness on the basis of their ethical conduct (p. 279). Silva (*JVN2*; 221-222) agrees that while "works of law" include ceremonial aspects, they cannot be reduced to them, and the reduced, narrower reading cannot be used as the hermeneutical key to the justification argument in Galatians.

O'Brien notes in a different chapter that (*JVN2*; 389) "according to Second Temple Judaism, David, like Abraham, was accepted by God and justified on the ground of his works." They were not accepted on the basis of their *ethnic distinctives*, but on the basis of their positive works. Paul's argument in Romans 4 is against the general position of Second Temple Judaism, which is why he demonstrates that neither Abraham nor David were justified on the basis of their works (Gathercole, *JVN2*; 160). They are both, according to Paul, examples of individuals who are justified *even though they are ungodly*. The issue with Abraham and David is ethical, not ethnic righteousness. Beyond that, David sinned, but offered atonement (which is what one must do in covenantal nomism). *But he was still ungodly.* He had the boundary markers, and he repented, but he was not considered righteous on that basis.

Douglas Moo, in his study of Romans 5-11, argues that "works of the law" is not just a technical phrase for boundary markers; they are a subset of general human works, and that is why they cannot justify (*JVN2*; 209-211). To invest the phrase with a technical meaning is not supported by Paul's usage. Moo further observes that in Paul's major treatment of the law, he does not refer to the law as a barrier which keeps Gentiles out: "Human inability, not Gentile exclusion, is the issue" (p. 208). Finally, Blocher (*JVN2*; 487) writes:

> Construing the phrase 'works of the law' to mean (or to re-fer to) only those works that were 'badges of Jewishness' flies in the face of all probabilities. Counter-arguments have proved decisive, and James D. G. Dunn himself has been led to qualify his earlier statements and to make significant concessions. The problem, in Romans 2, is the failure to obey the *ethical* precepts of the law – which failure produces the need for another way, without the works of the law. Replacing 'the law' in Galatians 3:21 by 'ceremonial regulations' verges on the absurd.

The old perspective's interpretation of the relationship between works and righteousness seems to these authors to still be a more accurate way to understand Paul than that proposed by the new perspective.

Wright's narrative of deliverance from exile is also weighed in the balance and found wanting by the contributors of *JVN2*. Moo (p. 188) suggests that when it comes to the interpretation of Romans, the new perspective has highlighted background issues at the expense of the foreground ones. Moo makes four strong points against Wright's view of exile:

> 1) The language used in post-exilic texts does not support the "continuing in exile" motif as a dominant theological category (p. 201).
>
> 2) The texts Wright uses to prove that the ongoing exile was found all through Second Temple Judaism do not demonstrate

what he thinks they do, and neither are they actually representative of all the different groups (pp. 201-202).

3) Rather than "continuing in exile" the texts are better understood through the familiar "already/not yet" tension. Israel had returned from exile, but the glorious promises of the post-exilic prophecies were only partially fulfilled; more would be coming in the future (p. 202).

4) Many individual Jews were satisfied with "their personal spiritual condition" (p. 202). Even if the Jews were collectively waiting for national glory, individually many were quite content with their righteousness and not looking for an exilic return.

O'Brien (*JVN2*; 285) finds himself in agreement with Moo. He writes: "First, there are serious, if not insurmountable problems with the view that Second Temple Judaism *as a whole* regarded the nation of Israel as still living in exile" (emphasis in original). O'Brien goes on to mention, however, that even if the exilic motif was dominant in Paul's time (which it wasn't), it would still have to be demonstrated that it is dominant in Paul's thinking and letters—which it is not (p. 285). O'Brien and Moo judge Wright to be wrong on two serious counts: in the first place, the "continuing in exile" motif is just not as widespread or as dominant in the thinking of Second Temple Judaism as he claims; and in the second place, it is not present in Paul's writing as an important category.

Besides the exilic motif, how have critical scholars responded to Wright's view of justification as covenant membership, or the recognition that someone is part of the covenant community (or *is* 'saved' to use popular terminology), rather than the traditional view that justification is how someone *becomes* saved? Piper in *The Future of Justification*

(2007; 90) points out that although Wright denies that Paul appeals to justification when he is talking about how someone can be saved, Romans 10:9-10 says otherwise. It is also the case that if "righteousness" is to be equated with "covenant membership," there is something strange about the many Israelites who were in the covenant but who were unrighteous (2007; p. 40; fn 7). In the end, Piper (2007) argues that Wright's definition of justification is unprecedented and full of confusion (pp. 44, 54-55). Most importantly, it does not make sense out of the texts. (In trying to keep this introduction an *introduction*, nothing more will be said at this point. I hope that this paragraph suffices as a point of departure into the fuller discussion.)

Works and Future Judgment

Another area that needs to be addressed is: what is the relationship between works and future judgment? As was noted above, the new perspective holds that the future judgment is based on works, and that these works are not merely evidential of salvation. O'Brien (*JVN2*; 269-270) finds serious inconsistencies with this view. The way it is presented, it does not end up being "a matter of God's work in Christ alone" (p. 270 fn 78). O'Brien recognizes that there are many passages which speak of judgment on the basis of works (p. 269) and is eager to uphold the reality that our works reveal who we really are (p. 270). Yet, "works are indispensable for they demonstrate the presence of true faith, and are evidence of one's being united with Christ in his death and resurrection" (p. 270). Even the works we do are on the basis of God's work (Eph. 2:8-10) and are only acceptable in Christ.

Piper agrees in spirit with O'Brien. In accord with all the creeds and confessions, Piper (2007; 110-115) holds that works are evidence of justification, but are in no way part of the basis of justification. Justification and sanctification are connected, but need to be kept separate; biblically, the latter grows out of the former (Piper, *Counted Righteous in Christ*, 2002; 71-79). Moral transformation, including works, is the evidence of justification, but must not be collapsed into justification. In Piper's estimation, Wright's position is ambiguous, and he cannot articulate the real relationship clearly (2007; 117-118). It seems that whenever works are—even partially—what justify us (rather than being evidence that we *have been justified*), the concept cannot be articulated without engendering confusion in regards to syngergism, semi-pelagianism, or the like. The question which needs to be satisfactorily answered is, "How can our works be part of our justification, without faith in Christ alone ceasing to be the final ground?" If justification is partly based on works, then it seems impossible for it to be fully based on faith in Christ.

Imputation

Lastly, a brief word on imputation: Wright is totally against the concept, and believes it is absurd to think of a judge passing his righteousness off to the defendant. Blocher (*JVN2*; 480) responds: "Minimal flexibility is enough to ward off this *reductio ad absurdum*: in no version of the Protestant view do believers receive the righteousness of God *as Judge*, the quality of his act of judgment (usually it is the righteousness of God the Son, our Mediator, in his obedience and atoning work for us)" (emphasis in original). Wright does not want one metaphor to improperly control theological thought when it comes to justification, but it seems that he is the one at this point who has pushed a metaphor beyond its bounds. We require an alien righteousness (*JVN2*; 495), and this alien righteousness is that of Christ, which cannot be distinguished from God's (pp. 498-499). It is not as the judge that God gives us righteousness; it is as the judge sees Christ's righteousness credited to us that he can pronounce the guilty justified. Wright makes the metaphor too wooden in the details.

Piper (2002; 41) defines imputation in the following way: "By *imputation* I am referring to the act in which God counts sinners to be righteousness through their faith in Christ on the basis of Christ's perfect 'blood and righteousness,' specifically the righteousness that Christ accomplished by his perfect obedience in life and death." Faith is not righteousness but it is instrumental. Although the New Testament does not specifically state that Christ's righteousness was imputed to us, it is just as necessary theologically as the doctrine of the Trinity according to Charles Hodge (Piper, 2002; 81 fn 26), and is a proper concept for systematic theology (D. A. Carson, in *Justification: What's at Stake in the Current Debates?* 2004). II Corinthians 5:21 and I Corinthians 1:30 are two passages which seem to require the imputation of Christ's righteousness.

Conclusion

I think it is only fair for me to offer my own perspective on the new perspective on justification. Just two tiny (but important) points will suffice. I do not do so in an attempt to convince, but only in an attempt to be honest about my own convictions in the matter for the sake of transparency. As much as we would like to think that our biases do not affect us, they often do more than we realize. Thus, our thinking can be disproportionate and skewed, even if unintentionally. And when our thinking is distorted in this way, then we can misrepresent others—again, even if unintentionally.

1. In my judgment, the biblical concept of justification is forensic, and it is the declaration that a guilty sinner is now legally considered innocent on the basis of faith alone in Christ's perfect atonement and righteousness. Justification is what brings us into the covenant community; it is not the recognition that we are already in it.

2. Works in future judgment provide evidence of our saving faith in Christ. It seems to me that the advocates of the new perspective cannot clearly or simply articulate their view without falling into traps on one side or the other which make Christ's perfect work less than complete and sufficient for our justification. My main concern here is less what the advocates of the new perspective *explicitly say*, than what the *implications* or *entailments* of their position actually are. I suspect the lack of clarity in this matter is owing to accepting a position, but not being able to accept its consequences. In other words, I think there is an internal, irrecon-

cilable tension in the new perspective at this point, but advocates are committed to both propositions. Explanations, then, inevitably come across as confusing and unclear, because clarity only reveals the problems that are inherent in the stance. Wright is on record as saying that Piper hasn't heard what he is saying, and that Carson doesn't understand the new perspective. Fair enough, but in my judgment this may be owing to the inability to understand anything that is lacking coherence.

Certainly much more has been said on this subject, and much more will be said. Again, at the risk of tedious over-repetition, this is really nothing more than a portal for entering the discussions. More data can be brought to bear from both directions. For example, I'm not convinced that leaving off all discussion on Philippians 3 was a good idea! But we need to stop somewhere, or else the pages run on and on, and a short introduction becomes just another large book (which, in my case, would be inferior to what's already available, and so an utter waste of time). I hope that by God's grace this was fairly representative, and that the balance between necessary over-simplification and unintentional distortion was accurate.

Works Cited

Carson, D. A. "The Vindication of Imputation: On Fields of Discourse and Semantic Fields." In *Justification: What's at Stake in the Current Debates?* ed. Mark Husbands and Daniel Treier, 46-78. Downers Grove: InterVarsity Press, 2004.

Carson, D. A., Peter O'Brien, and Mark Seifrid, ed. *Justification and Variegated Nomism, Volume 1: The Complexities of Second Temple Judaism*. Grand Rapids: Baker, 2001.

Carson, D. A., Peter O'Brien, and Mark Seifrid, ed. *Justification and Variegated Nomism, Volume 2: The Paradoxes of Paul*. Grand Rapids: Baker, 2004.

Dunn, James D. G. *The New Perspective on Paul, Revised Edition*. Grand Rapids: Eerdmans, 2008.

Garlington, Don. *In Defense of the New Perspective on Paul: Essays and Reviews*. Eugene, OR: Wipf & Stock, 2005.

Piper, John. *The Future of Justification: A Response to N. T. Wright*. Wheaton, IL: Crossway, 2007.

Piper, John. *Counted Righteous in Christ: Should We Abandon the Imputation of Christ's Righteousness?* Wheaton, IL: Crossway, 2002.

Sanders, E. P. *Paul*. New York: Sterling, 2009.

Sanders, E. P. *Paul and Palestinian Judaism*. Philadelphia: Fortress Press, 1977.

Wright, N. T. *Justification: God's Plan & Paul's Vision*. Downers Grove, IL: InterVarsity Press, 2009.

www.ingramcontent.com/pod-product-compliance
Lightning Source LLC
Chambersburg PA
CBHW071644040426
42452CB00009B/1763